RED, WHITE, AND BLUE

OUR FLAG MATTERS TO ME AND YOU!

A children's book about why we stand for our American flag
and some of the many freedoms it represents.

by DR. BEN CARSON
with VALERIE PFUNDSTEIN

Illustrated by JUSTIN LOUIS

To the men, women, and families
who have sacrificed to give us freedom and
those who honor our flag, which represents them.
—B. C.

To students who salute our flag every morning,
reminding us to begin each day with humble hearts.
—V. P.

To my boy.
—J.L.

That flag shouldn't be on the ground.
It shouldn't be all in tatters.
Please respect it as it deserves.
Let me explain why it matters.

When you see our flag, it's special.
Take a moment to stop and stare.
Enjoy its design and beauty,
and think about why it is there.

The thirteen stripes, the fifty stars,
and the colors red, white, and blue,
were put together on a flag,
Especially for me and you!

Red and white stripes are one for each
colony that first cleared the way.
All the white stars are one for each
of the states that we have today.

When sewn carefully together,
the flag waves proudly and unfurled
to symbolize all our freedoms
that are known throughout the world.

We show our respect for the flag.
It's an emblem of our nation.
Place hand on heart, or in salute,
and stand in appreciation.

We stand because we're free to lead
those who might need a helpful guide.
We assist them on their journey
as we walk along, side by side.

We lead others throughout the world,
in countries near and far away,
to help them in their times of need,
and get them back along their way.

We stand because we're free to care
for all in our community.
Providing treatment for our friends
is a way to show unity.

Doctors, nurses, and scientists
offer to travel anywhere.
If someone, somewhere, needs their help,
our Americans will be there.

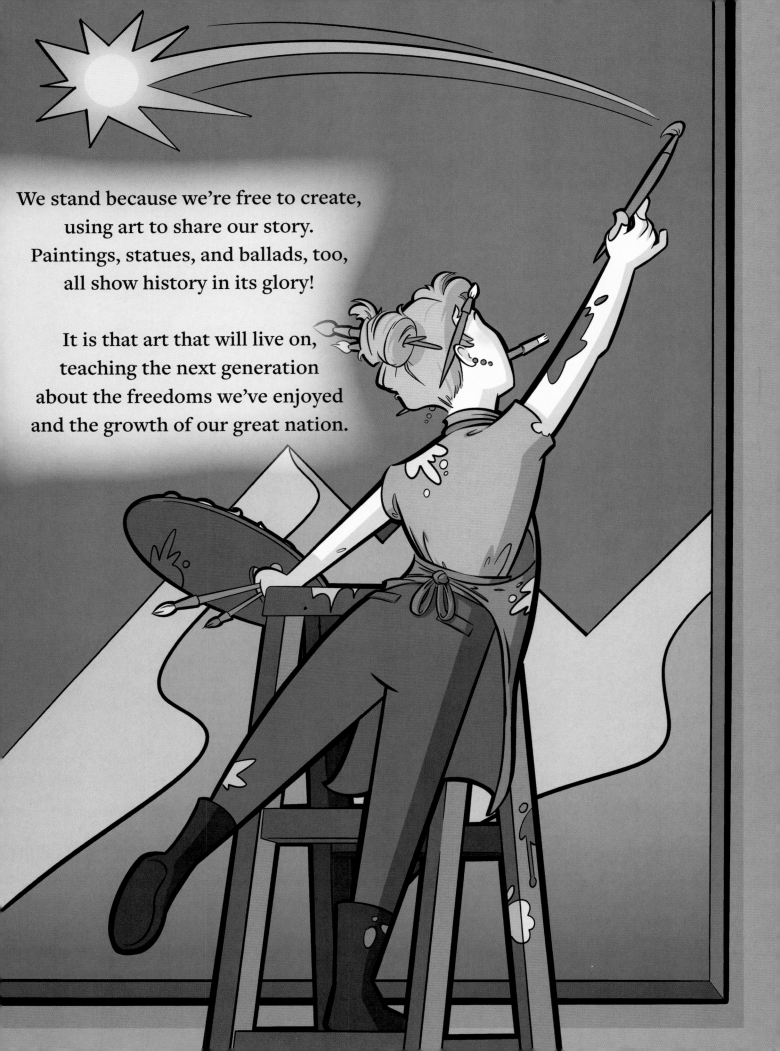

We stand because we're free to create,
using art to share our story.
Paintings, statues, and ballads, too,
all show history in its glory!

It is that art that will live on,
teaching the next generation
about the freedoms we've enjoyed
and the growth of our great nation.

We stand because we're free to compete,
becoming faster and stronger,
challenging ourselves and others
to jump higher and run longer.

From the historical records
to the individual feats,
sometimes the personal milestones
matter the most to our athletes.

We stand because we're free to vote
and choose who will represent us.
They, in turn, speak on our behalf
to make choices, some momentous!

Each and everyone's vote matters,
one person, one vote to be fair.
It doesn't matter who you are,
find your voting place and be there!

We stand because we're free to explore
from the depths to the greatest heights,
from our backyard to outer space,
taking adventures to new sites.

When we explore we're learning more
about the world all around us.
And then we want to go further
through the unknown that surrounds us.

We stand because we're free to grow,
 tilling soil and then planting seed.
We tend to the earth and farmlands
 to produce the crops that we need.

Our farmers grow and raise food we eat,
 livestock, vegetables, and fruits, too.
It's then delivered to markets
 where we buy food as we're used to.

We stand because we're free to speak,
no matter what we want to say.
We can speak in homes and outside,
any day or place, it's okay!

We can speak to support causes,
or we can peacefully oppose.
Either way, our voices are heard.
That's the way America goes!

We stand because we're free to dream
without anyone else's permission.
Hard work makes our dreams possible
when we choose our own ambition.

We can dream about our futures,
and to make the world better too,
like leaders of our country's past
whose dreams continue to come true.

We stand because we're free to defend
in the name of our great nation.
Men and women in uniform
preserve our country's foundation.

Some Americans that defend
serve on land, at sea, and in air,
to fight for freedoms of others
throughout the world... no matter where.

We stand because we're free to build,
our country's growing every day,
tall buildings, schools, and even parks,
where we work, go to school, and play.

Our builders and our engineers
travel the world to share their skills.
They help others build their structures,
build bridges, and even windmills.

We stand because we're free to pray
to follow the faith of our choice.
We pray where, when, and how we want...
another way we use our voice.

It's only in prayer that we kneel
when it's our faith's expectation.
We kneel to God, but stand for the flag
in loyalty to our nation.

We stand because we're free to protect
and keep others safe from dangers.
We protect our families at home
and children away from strangers.

Our community protectors,
from the firefighters to police,
protect our lives and our houses,
and keep our neighborhoods at peace.

We stand because we're free to travel
to the destinations we choose.
We can go wherever we want
on roads, in flight, by train, or cruise.

We travel to homes of neighbors
and to friends that live far away,
without requesting permission
from anyone along the way.

We stand because we're free to invent,
to build a mousetrap that's better.
What might simplify YOUR own life?
Invent it! Be a go-getter!

Some inventions can be simple,
others are more complicated,
but all of them improve our lives
and phase out what is outdated.

We stand because we're free to share,
thanks to our freedom of the press,
writing, broadcasting, blogging, too,
sharing both freely and fearless.

Sharing the news as you see it
can be very challenging, too,
since we see the world differently
depending on our point of view.

We stand because we're free to learn
no matter where we may come from.
No one limits what we can learn
and what we think we can become.

Our teachers are always ready
to teach us ideas old and new,
preparing us for our futures
no matter what we choose to do.

We stand because we're free to agree
and compare commonalities.
It's possible to think alike
with different personalities.

Even though we're free to agree,
we're free to also disagree.
We can learn from one another
if we're listening carefully.

Standing together shows respect
even if we may disagree,
because that flag waves for us all
reminding us that we are free.

THE PLEDGE OF ALLEGIANCE

I pledge allegiance
to the flag
of the United States of America,
and to the republic
for which it stands,
one nation under God,
indivisible,
with liberty
and justice for all.

This 13-fold procedure was common long before the more modern assigned meanings. The source and date of origin of the meanings is unknown, but the 13 meanings can create an uplifting experience.

This is one version of what the **13 folds** mean:

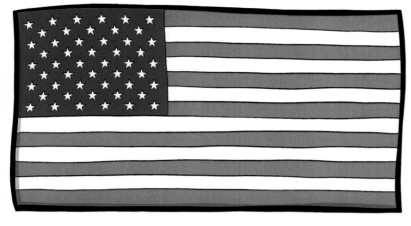

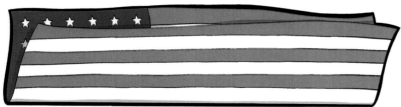

The **first fold** of our flag is a symbol of life.
Fold the lower striped section of the flag over the blue field.

The **second fold** signifies our belief in eternal life.
Folded edge is then folded over to meet the open edge.

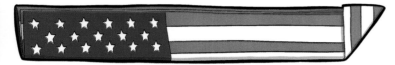

The **third fold** is made in honor and tribute to veterans.
A triangular fold is then started by bringing the striped corner of the folded edge to the open edge.

The **fourth fold** exemplifies our trust in God.
Outer point is then turned inward parallel with the open edge to form a second triangle.

The **fifth fold** is an acknowledgment to our country.
Triangular folding is continued until the entire length of the flag is folded in the triangular shape with only the blue field visible.

The **sixth fold** is for where our hearts lie.

The **seventh fold** is a tribute to our armed forces.

The **eighth fold** is a tribute to those who have passed away.

The **ninth fold** is an honor to motherhood.

The **10th fold** is a tribute to fatherhood.

The **11th fold** glorifies God.

The **12th fold** represents an emblem of eternity.

The **last fold** reminds us of our national motto, "In God We Trust."

Completed

About the American Cornerstone Institute

Red, White, and Blue: Our Flag Matters to Me and You is part of the Little Patriots program produced by non-profit organization, the American Cornerstone Institute (ACI). This is the second book by the Little Patriots program, preceded by *Why America Matters* released in 2021.

ACI was founded by world-renowned neurosurgeon, Dr. Ben Carson, and is guided by the cornerstones of Faith, Liberty, Community, and Life in its work to strengthen the bonds that hold our country together through educational programs for Americans of all ages. You can view Little Patriots' cartoon series and download free educational materials for children via www.littlepatriotslearning.com.

SCAN TO LEARN MORE ▸

LITTLE PATRIOTS

AMERICAN CORNERSTONE INSTITUTE

Faith. Liberty. Community. Life.